Hope for the Grieving Spouse

Turning Ashes to Diamonds

Linda (Swinderman) Cronebaugh

WESTBOW PRESS®
A DIVISION OF THOMAS NELSON
& ZONDERVAN

Copyright © 2017 Linda (Swinderman) Cronebaugh.

All rights reserved. No part of this book may be used or reproduced by any means, graphic, electronic, or mechanical, including photocopying, recording, taping or by any information storage retrieval system without the written permission of the author except in the case of brief quotations embodied in critical articles and reviews.

Scripture quotations marked (NIV) are taken from the Holy Bible, New International Version®, NIV®. Copyright © 1973, 1978, 1984, 2011 by Biblica, Inc.™ Used by permission of Zondervan. All rights reserved worldwide. www.zondervan.com The "NIV" and "New International Version" are trademarks registered in the United States Patent and Trademark Office by Biblica, Inc.™

Scripture quotations marked (NIrV) are taken from the Holy Bible, New International Reader's Version®, NIrV® Copyright © 1995, 1996, 1998, 2014 by Biblica, Inc.™ Used by permission of Zondervan. All rights reserved worldwide. www.zondervan.com The "NIrV" and "New International Reader's Version" are trademarks registered in the United States Patent and Trademark Office by Biblica, Inc.™

Scripture taken from the New Century Version®. Copyright © 2005 by Thomas Nelson. Used by permission. All rights reserved.

Scripture taken from the New King James Version®. Copyright © 1982 by Thomas Nelson. Used by permission. All rights reserved.

WestBow Press books may be ordered through booksellers or by contacting:

WestBow Press

A Division of Thomas Nelson & Zondervan
1663 Liberty Drive
Bloomington, IN 47403
www.westbowpress.com
1 (866) 928-1240

Because of the dynamic nature of the Internet, any web addresses or links contained in this book may have changed since publication and may no longer be valid. The views expressed in this work are solely those of the author and do not necessarily reflect the views of the publisher, and the publisher hereby disclaims any responsibility for them.

Any people depicted in stock imagery provided by Thinkstock are models, and such images are being used for illustrative purposes only.

Certain stock imagery © Thinkstock.

ISBN: 978-1-5127-8629-3 (sc)
ISBN: 978-1-5127-8631-6 (hc)
ISBN: 978-1-5127-8630-9 (e)

Library of Congress Control Number: 2017906927

Print information available on the last page.

WestBow Press rev. date: 05/12/2017

This book is dedicated to God the glorious, who has led me *through*.

God's promise in Isaiah 43:2 (NIV *emphasis added*) is this: "When you pass *through* the waters, I will be with you; And when you pass *through* the rivers, they will not sweep over you. When you walk *through* the fire, you will not be burned. The flames will not set you ablaze."

"This tender and hope-filled devotional and prayer collection will help you grieve honestly and openly. It invites you to bring to God your hurts and to receive the love from God that will move you from coping to healing."

—Delinda Grindle, grief counselor

"Linda takes us through her own intimate journey with grief. This devotional helps us deal with practical, everyday occurrences where the uninvited guest grief intrudes on our life. *Hope for the Grieving Spouse* is both comforting and God-honoring."

—Jan Shackleton, widow

"I will always remember the night fifteen years ago when Linda came to my door. My husband, Gene, had died suddenly after a long-term spinal cord injury. She was there to offer solace, love, friendship, and prayer. We had been friends for several years and bonded over caring for disabled husbands. God has blessed Linda with a compassionate nature that empathizes with people. In *Hope for the Grieving Spouse* she offers insights in each chapter to encourage us to grieve at our own pace, with suggestions to get through each day, week, month, and year. Especially meaningful are the scriptures and prayers at the end of a chapter. Linda has walked life's journey with her hand firmly in God's—and she gently leads us to walk with God, who lovingly holds us in His hands."

—Judith Beard, widow

Contents

Acknowledgments xi

Introduction 1
Allow Yourself to Grieve 5
Cold Nights 9
The Firsts 13
Inappropriate Feelings 17
My Life Is Out of Control 21
Accept a Good Support System 25
Do I Need a Grief Counselor or a Grief Support
Group? 29
Stay in Tune with God! 33
Hygiene and Housekeeping Are Different For You 37
The Bedroom 41
Going Back to Church 45
Changes, Selling the House, Moving 49
Why Am I Still Here? 53
The Presence 57
Cleaning Out the Closet 61
Who Am I Now? 65

Laughing Again... 69
"You Are Not Over This Yet?" 73
When Will Everything Be Normal Again? 77
Special Remembrance Days 79

Conclusion.. 83
Appendix... 87

Acknowledgments

I wish to acknowledge some very special people without whom I could not have accomplished the task of writing *Hope for the Grieving Spouse*. I first must thank my son, Cory; his wife, Rachel Swinderman; and my grandchildren. Cory has been an amazing son through the twenty-five-year illness of Tom, his father, and then the loss of Tom and my second husband, Dave. Together, Cory and his family have given me loving support, including finding me a grief counselor after Dave's passing.

To my stepchildren, Jason and Rachel Cronebaugh, who continue to love me and think of me as family.

To my brother and his wife, Larry and NJ Speece, for their support and belief in *Hope for the Grieving Spouse*.

To my father, Walter Speece, who is also on this grief journey after the passing of my mother and who has found hope within these pages.

To my grief counselor, Delinda Grindle, for suggesting to me the need for a book like this and encouraging me to write it.

To my friend Jan Shackleton, who diligently encouraged me to write this book and has been my "grammar guru."

To the many other family and friends who have walked these grief journeys with me, and have supported and loved me through my good and not-so-good days.

And to my heavenly Father, who daily has guided me. He promises in His Word, "I will never leave you nor forsake you" (Josh. 1:5b NIV). He has definitely kept that promise to me. Without Him, *Hope for the Grieving Spouse* would be a bunch of words on a page, but with Him, it is words that bring hope!

● ● ● ● ● ● ● ● ● ● ●

Introduction

As I sit here in the favorite chair of my departed spouse, I picture you sitting in or near the chair of the spouse whom you lost. The feelings that you have are almost beyond description, but let me try to describe them. You feel an extreme pain in your chest, or even your entire body. That pain may present itself in many ways: a feeling of being lost, a feeling that you can't go on with life, or feelings of frustration, depression, hopelessness, or even anger. Your body may even feel paralyzed. You may feel like you can't get out of bed in the morning or even out of the chair you are in right now. Putting one foot in front of the other seems impossible and takes extreme strength. Some of you may find yourselves frequently wrapped in your spouse's favorite blanket or piece of clothing.

May I say to you that all of the above things are normal for those who have suffered a loss as great as yours! You have likely lost your best friend. Some of you had been with your spouse for only a short time while others had been with their spouses for many years. No matter the amount of time, your spouse was someone you loved deeply and miss immensely.

May I also say that this feeling of hopelessness, and the thought that you cannot go on, will not last forever! You will one day have hope again. You will one day desire to continue life and envision a future for yourself. Right now, though, this seems impossible.

You are beginning a journey—a grief journey. I personally have made that journey twice. The first time was after my first husband died of multiple sclerosis, an illness he'd had for twenty-five years. The second time was after my second husband fell and suffered a severe brain injury; he passed away a week later. Each of these grief journeys was different. Each left me a different person, a stronger person, and I believe, a better person, with God's help.

I am praying that God will be our guide as we begin our grief journeys together. May God use these devotionals to bring *hope* back into your life!

● ● ● ● ● ● ● ● ● ● ●

Scripture

"By day the Lord directs his love, at night his song is with me—a prayer to the God of my life" (Ps. 42:8 NIV).

Prayer

Let the Lord embrace you in His arms today! Amen.

Allow Yourself to Grieve

The service is completed. Family and friends have gone back to their own lives. You have opened all the cards. Now you are left alone! This is the time when the paralysis seems the greatest. You have no idea what to do. You try to think, but you cannot concentrate on anything specific for any length of time. The easiest thing to do is to sit in that special chair, wrapped in that special blanket or piece of clothing that once belonged to your spouse, and do nothing else. You feel safe in that spot. It will be the spot you will return to many times over the next months and maybe even years.

As you sit in your safe spot, please make one important decision: *I am going to allow myself to grieve.* That grieving time has no certain limit. It has no certain format for you to follow. It will be determined by the circumstances of your spouse's death, your personality, your age, and even your relationship with God. There is no book out there that will tell you exactly how to do your grieving. (However, there are many good books out there to help you.) It will all depend on you and your willingness to allow yourself to grieve.

After the death of my first husband, I did not follow this advice very well. At the ten-month mark, I became very ill. Then I allowed myself to grieve some. After the death of my second husband, I said, "I want to be healthy when I come through this." I allowed myself to grieve. Much of what I share in the following sections comes from that statement, "I want to be healthy when I come through this."

The million-dollar questions today are as follows: Will you allow yourself to grieve? Will you take care of yourself during your grieving? Will you allow yourself the amount of time needed to grieve? Do you desire to be healthy when you reach the plateau of your grieving? (You will never stop missing your spouse or even grieving his or her loss, but you will reach a place where the grieving is less and living becomes greater.)

* * * * * * * * * * *

Scripture

"No one whose *hope* is in you, will ever be put to shame" (Ps. 25:3a NIV, emphasis added).

Prayer

Father God, I pray for those who read this devotional. I pray that You will wrap them in Your loving arms and that they will sense Your presence near to them. May they see a glimmer of hope as they reach out to You! In Jesus's name I pray, amen.

Cold Nights

For me this did not happen right away, but one night once I went to bed alone, I could not get warm. I was literally shaking from feeling cold. I got up and put on an extra layer of clothes, some gloves, and a pair of socks, and added more blankets. I realized I was entirely alone. My spouse was not there. The bed was completely empty. The body heat of my spouse was missing. I slept the whole night covered with these extra clothes and blankets! In fact, I slept this way for several nights. Eventually there came a time when I did not need the extra coverings to stay warm.

Feeling cold at night is not unusual for someone who is grieving his or her spouse. For some, an empty bed is a really hard thing to face because they have slept wrapped in their partners' arms each night for years. For others, their time of sleeping may not have been a touching time, but they knew that the other person was there—by their snoring, by the noise of their CPAP or BPAP machine, or by just the rhythm of their breathing. But mostly they knew by the warmth of their spouses' bodies.

After my husband died, I started sleeping with a cute little stuffed panda bear. The panda bear had significance to my husband. The bear has become so special in my family that my two-year-old grandchild talks about and carries around Grandma Linda's bear. I am sure that when she tells the mailman that this is Grandma Linda's bear, he is thinking, *What?* But that is okay. My desire is to be healthy! I have committed to doing whatever it takes to accomplish that goal—even sporting a stuffed animal!

What are you willing to do to help ease the feeling of loneliness at night in that big bed? Some find peace by changing to a twin bed. The large bed for them brings back too many memories that are hard to overcome. There is no right answer to the question. You do what works best for you. The key here is for you to be healthy!

* * * * * * * * * *

Scripture

Picture with me the children around Jesus. You are one of those children—maybe a little older and bigger, but one of God's children nonetheless. And you hear Jesus say these words: "Let the children come to me and do not hinder them," followed by the description, "And Jesus took the children in his arms" (Mark 10:14b, 16a NIV). Now, my friend, let Jesus put His arms around you today. Crawl up in His lap and be held by your amazing friend!

Prayer

Father God, may Your children feel Your loving arms surrounding them. May You ease the pain and emptiness they are feeling, and may they feel instead Your amazing love and hope for them. In Jesus's name, amen.

The Firsts

When we think of the first year after the death of a spouse when all of the firsts happen, most of the time we think of the first Christmas, the first Thanksgiving, the first anniversary, the first birthday, and the first Valentine's Day. Those are all days that likely were very important to you and your spouse. But the days I found hardest were those I hadn't expected to be hard or to be a first for me.

My spouse and I traveled a lot for the company that employed him. About six weeks after my spouse's passing, on my grandson's birthday, I awoke with a feeling I didn't expect. I should have been happy and excited to go and celebrate with my family. But I wasn't. I could hardly get out of bed. I went to my safe place, the chair; wrapped myself in the blanket; and cried and cried. What I hadn't thought about was that I was going to travel for the first time out of town by myself, and I would be going to my grandson's birthday party without Grandpa Dave. I had not seen this as a problem until I awoke that morning. I was blindsided. The paralysis I felt was intense. I didn't think I could put one foot in front of the other. I called my son. I didn't know if I could make this trip, but I did not want to disappoint my grandson. I did eventually make the trip, but I kept the blanket on the seat next to me in the car. I touched it many times as I drove down the road.

I don't know how your firsts will be. I don't know which one or ones will be the hardest. I don't know which days will actually become one of your firsts. But I do know that you will have to do those firsts your own way. You will need to approach those days in the way you feel most comfortable. It may be that you will miss a few of those days and remain seated in your safe place at home—and that is okay. The goal is for you to be healthy—whatever that entails for you!

● ● ● ● ● ● ● ● ● ● ●

Scripture

"But you, O Lord, are a compassionate and gracious God. Slow to anger, abounding in love and faithfulness" (Ps. 86:15 NIV). As you approach each of your firsts, remember the God we serve. He is not pushing you; He is walking along beside you. He feels your pain, and He desires to patiently guide you as you walk through these days. He is not out to belittle you or make you feel bad in any way. He is "compassionate and gracious ... slow to anger ... abounding in love and faithfulness" (Ps. 86:15 NIV).

Prayer

Father God, may You lead these dear bereaved spouses as they face each of their firsts. May You bring people to them who will not push them but who will be kind and gracious to them! May they be blessed with someone to stand by them during their firsts! In Jesus's name, amen.

Inappropriate Feelings

It was the day of visitation for my first husband. My son's best friend came to where I was sitting and related his feelings to me. By the look on his face, I could tell he was very troubled. He said to me, "I have this feeling of relief that Tom has died. It's over! But I feel guilty thinking like this." I understood. It was the same feeling my son and I had had a few nights earlier when we walked out of the nursing home for the last time. My spouse—his father—had just passed after a battle with multiple sclerosis that lasted twenty-five years. The battle was over! My spouse—his father—was free of the ravages of MS! Relief? I didn't think it was inappropriate.

Another feeling sometimes thought inappropriate is that of joyfulness—laughing and having fun. Your feeling of real joy will probably not come right away, but someday you will have joy and laugh again. Until then, you need to laugh and try to have fun. These are not inappropriate goals. Your spouse would desire for you to be joyful and happy. "Weeping may remain for a night, but rejoicing comes in the morning" (Ps. 30:5 NIV).

Hope? You have got to be kidding! How can I have hope? Look at what I am going through. Look at what has just happened. Oh, how I remember disliking this passage. "For I know the plans I have for you, declares the Lord. Plans to prosper you and not to harm you. Plans to give you *hope* and a future" (Jer. 29:11 NIV, emphasis added). During the time when I was grieving my first husband, someone gave me a mug with this passage of scripture on it. I looked at my secret Santa and said, "Yeah, right!" I was mean, and I wish I hadn't been, but hope was an inappropriate feeling to me at that time. I will say, though, that this verse has become my motto during the grieving of my second husband. I believe God has a hope and a future for me!

Are these feelings and others like them inappropriate? I don't think so. And these feelings will not last forever. They are stepping-stones that we step on as we travel our personal grief journeys. Your inappropriate feelings may be different from mine, but yours are very important to you. Confront your feelings, and in so doing find health.

● ● ● ● ● ● ● ● ● ●

Prayer

Father God, I pray for the special people who are struggling with these feelings and others we have not listed. May they not be deceived into believing these feelings are inappropriate, but instead may they see them as stepping-stones leading toward positive growth in their grief journeys. Guide them, O great Jehovah. Amen.

* * * * * * * * * *

My Life Is Out of Control

It is days, and maybe weeks or even months, after the funeral. You are trying to settle back into a routine. Previously you may have been someone who lived by lists, or you may have been a very organized person—or maybe organization never has been your thing—but now you find that you cannot find a daily routine.

You wake up wondering, *What should be on my agenda today?* If you are a person who has a job, this will not be as much of an issue, but if you do not have employment or are retired, this can be a real problem. You get up with an unsettled feeling and find yourself trying to plan your day. You may be paralyzed in the chair and find it impossible even to get going, or you may start doing something only to jump to something else. Nothing gets completed. Your day ends with feelings of confusion, just as it began.

This is another step in the grief journey. Your mind and your body are trying to cope with your intense loss. Adding organization or planning to your life creates an overload. This will not last forever. There is hope that you will find a routine again.

For me, I eventually designated certain days when I would leave the house—my outside-the-home days. I would save all of my errands, meetings, appointments, etc., and accomplish them in that one or possibly two days. In my mind, I knew I had a home day the next day, which gave me the motivation to accomplish the outside-the-home agenda on that day. Even after two years, I still use this method. It has become very helpful to me.

But you may say, "I am a parent of young children"; or "I have a very intense job"; or "I have extended family requirements and what I am reading doesn't fit my circumstances." In such cases, I do not have a complete answer for you, but I do want to say that after the death of my first husband, I had a full-time job and many commitments. I pushed myself, and in so doing, I did not take care of myself. I was not healthy following his death. I pray that you will ask for help from those around you. People do care and desire to help, but many times they do not know how to help. Ask for *specific* help!

* * * * * * * * * * *

Scripture

"The steps of a good man are ordered by the Lord, and He delights in his way" (Ps. 37:23 NKJV). God delights in and is captivated by every detail of our lives!

Prayer

Father, give direction and guidance to these bereaved spouses. Show them how to bring some order to their confusion. Amen.

Accept a Good Support System

● ● ● ● ● ● ● ● ● ●

Praise be to the God and Father of our Lord Jesus Christ, the Father of compassion and the God of all comfort, *who comforts us in all our troubles, so that we can comfort those in any trouble* with the comfort we ourselves have received from God.

—2 Cor. 1:3–4 (NIV, emphasis added)

Think about some special people in your life. Who are they? Why do you consider them special? Have they walked in your shoes? Have they experienced loss as you have?

It amazes me the number of times I have heard these words: "I believe God is telling me to talk to you." It amazes me how many times people, without knowing my first husband had MS, have come up to me and asked, "Do you know anything about MS?" In each of these types of situations, God has placed me in the path of someone who has lost a spouse, been diagnosed with MS, or sees me as someone with whom they need to talk. I believe this is why God has led me to write this book!

Friends, there are people around you who can be a great support system for you. They may be friends; they may be someone new who drops into your life; they may be a neighbor; they may be someone at your church. Look for them. When you feel God's nudge, go to them and ask to talk to them. Maybe you could invite them over for coffee or out to lunch. Again, your comfort is important.

Remember, not everyone will be good as part of your support system. Some people mean well but, not having experienced a loss, may do more harm than good. Seek God's direction as you build your support system.

* * * * * * * * * * *

Prayer

Father, I pray that You will guide these spouses to wonderful people who will be a support to them through their grieving journeys. May You direct this spouse to just the right person or people for him or her. Amen.

● ● ● ● ● ● ● ● ● ●

Do I Need a Grief Counselor or a Grief Support Group?

I remember my answer to the question asked by the bereavement director at the hospice after the death of my first husband: "No, I don't need counseling. I am doing just fine." I wasn't doing well, and she knew that. She had been watching me (we went to the same church). The day she called, I was at home ill with pneumonia. After I hung up the phone, God began to talk to me and nudge me, saying, "You need help!" So I called the bereavement counselor back and signed up for the next grief support group sessions.

I wish I could say I entered those sessions desiring help. I did not. I entered with a chip on my shoulder. I didn't want to be there, but knew I needed to be. I wished there was some way I could skip this part of my grieving journey.

Looking back on the sessions and the book we used, I am very glad I took the time and made the sessions a part of my grieving journey. What I wish is that I hadn't entered the sessions with such resistance. I could have received more help had I allowed myself to truly enter this part of my grief journey.

After the death of my second husband, I entered grief counseling through a service at the funeral home. This time I approached the process with a different attitude. The sixteen months I spent with the grief counselor there were very valuable for me. I know I would not have written *Hope for the Grieving Spouse* had I not made the time for grief counseling during my grief journey. Grieving my second husband's death compelled me to regrieve my first husband's death.

Yes, friend, you do need to seek grief counseling. Sometimes this service is offered through a funeral home, but it is always offered through hospice. There are also private counselors. Two important questions to ask when seeking a private counselor: Does the counselor's education include specialization in grief counseling? Is the counselor a follower of Jesus?

Grief counseling is another important avenue to bring hope into your life again! "I pray also that the eyes of your heart may be enlightened in order that you may know the hope to which he has called you" (Eph. 1:18 NIV).

* * * * * * * * * *

Prayer

Father, please give this spouse the courage to seek and accept counseling as he or she walks this grief journey. Guide him or her to a counselor and/or group that will bring hope into his or her life. Amen.

● ● ● ● ● ● ● ● ● ● ●

Stay in Tune with God!

This is probably not the best time to decide to read the Bible from cover to cover in a year. In fact, it may be hard for you to read the Bible and pray. It is not that you don't love God as you did before your loss, but it may be that you are struggling with anger and wanting answers to the why questions.

Oh, I know that we serve a sovereign God and that all things work together for good, but I don't want to hear that today. I have lost. I have suffered a humongous loss. I am angry, and I have many questions. After my second husband's death, I responded to people in the following way: *"Not again!"* "Why did this happen?" "Why do I have to suffer this *again*?" "He and I had been married only a little over four years. We were just to the point of understanding each other's quirks. Life was good! *Why?*"

When we read the psalms, we find David many times crying out to God in anger, hurt, and frustration. God never turned His back on David. He loved David. In fact, it is said of David that "the Lord has sought out a man after his own heart" (1 Sam. 13:14 NIV). Those times when David lashed out brought him closer to God. David said, "I am still confident of this; I will see the goodness of the Lord in the land of the living" (Ps. 27:13 NIV). David found hope in the midst of his troubles.

God has broad shoulders. When we cry out to Him in anger and frustration, He cries along with us. He cares about us very much. He doesn't want us to hurt or suffer loss, but we do hurt and suffer because of sin. (Sin wasn't part of God's plan.) Read this verse several times: "But you, O Lord, are a compassionate and gracious God, slow to anger, *abounding in love and faithfulness*" (Ps. 86:15 NIV, emphasis added).

Be encouraged, my friend. You will have hope again. You will again "rejoice in your salvation" (Ps. 30:5b NIV). You will not always have negative feelings, and "God will never leave you nor forsake you" (Josh. 1:5 NIV) as you travel through the storm!

* * * * * * * * * *

Prayer

Father, reveal Your glory to this precious spouse. May this spouse see *Your hand* guiding him or her to the days of hope that are coming! You are a loving and faithful God. Thank You, Jesus. Amen

● ● ● ● ● ● ● ● ● ● ●

Hygiene and Housekeeping Are Different For You

When was the last time you took a shower? Washed your hair? Changed your bed clothes? Ran the sweeper? Dusted the furniture? I don't ask these things to put guilt on your shoulders. I ask because if it has been a while since you've done any of these things, or if you do them less frequently than you used to, I want you to know that this is a normal thing in the grief journey. Depending on the length of time since your loss, getting out of a chair may still be a difficult task, let alone taking care of yourself or your dwelling.

Again, whether or not a grieving spouse attends to personal hygiene and does housekeeping will be different depending on whether or not you are employed or unemployed (including being retired). I had no problem with hygiene and housekeeping after my first husband's death, but I really had a struggle after my second husband's death. I still find it comforting to have those "no shower; still in my PJs" days every once in a while.

The key here is not to allow these actions to become your normal, everyday routine. As I said earlier, I had some at-home days, but I also had my out-of-the-house days when I had to shower, dress, and face the schedule for the day. When I first started having out-of-the-house days, I actually had friends drive me from place to place. Since I found it hard to concentrate, I knew it was safer for me and those drivers around me if I had a driver. (This is one specific area someone can help you with.)

I know from movies and from hearing personal stories that many times well-meaning friends walk into our homes, see us still in our PJs, and think, *I have got to get her [or him] out of here.* These well-meaning friends believe that the best thing for the grieving spouse is to get the person to take a shower, get dressed, and get out of the house. But that is not always the best thing. Maybe it is best for the grieving spouse to have her or his time and space in that unshowered, PJ-wearing state. Tomorrow or the next day may be his or her "cleaned up and out of the house" day.

Someday the saying "cleanliness is next to godliness" may again have meaning to you, but for today be good to yourself. Remember, you are striving to be healthy when you reach the next level of your grief journey. (I would say "when you reach the end of your grief journey," but that time never really comes. We just reach the next level, and the next level, and the next level.) Whatever it takes for you to reach a place of health, please do it.

My friend, "Be strong and courageous. Do not be terrified; do not be discouraged, for the Lord your God will be with you wherever you go" (Josh. 1:9 NIV). He is with you right now!

● ● ● ● ● ● ● ● ● ●

Prayer

Father, bless these spouses today with Your amazing presence and peace. Give them assurance that You will help them and will never, ever leave them. There is hope! Amen.

The Bedroom

You and your spouse's bedroom has a special meaning that is yours and yours alone. For some grieving spouses, the bedroom once was a place where love was shared and enjoyed, but for others, the bedroom may bring back an altogether different set of memories. Ultimately, though, the bedroom was a place shared by two very special people with a special bond.

Now one of those special people is gone. The bond has been broken by death. Walking into the bedroom now does not bring the comfort it once did. In fact, the feelings now may be sad. Walking into the bedroom can be emotional and even overwhelming. What can you do to help yourself cope with this room and that area of your life?

For me, after each of my spouses died, I found it very important to make the bedroom mine. It was no longer ours. *When you are ready*, make the bedroom yours by rearranging furniture if you can (I put my husband's side of the bed against the wall so no one could get in on that side) and redecorating (I gave the bedroom a feminine touch). But you are not me. You may desire to move from your side of the bed to your spouse's side of the bed. You may wish to keep things in the bedroom that remind you of you and your spouse together. (I have a picture of my first husband and me on our wedding day on my dresser, as well as a picture of my second husband and me cutting our wedding cake.) In both times of death, I made the bedroom *my* bedroom, setting it up and decorating the way I wanted it. If it is financially feasible, you may want to start all over with a whole new bedroom. Only you know what works best for you.

As we close this section, I want to pray a special prayer for each of you. Some of you will desire to marry again, and some will say, "No way. Never." Either way is okay. I desired to remarry after the death of my first husband, but now that my second husband has died, I am not sure if I will marry again.

● ● ● ● ● ● ● ● ● ● ●

Prayer

Father, I lift each spouse to You. For each one You have plans to prosper and not to harm; plans for *hope* and a *future*. Guide each one to *Your best!* In Jesus's name, amen.

• • • • • • • • • •

Going Back to Church

Have you gone back to church yet? If you haven't, why do you find it a hard thing to do? Did you and your spouse frequently attend church, perhaps going weekly? Was it the place where you met your spouse? Was it the place where your spouse's funeral was held? Is it a place where tears seem to flow more heavily? Are you not ready to answer the many people who ask "How are you?" Do you find it difficult to respond when someone at church says, "We have been missing you." or "Where have you been? It's been six months. Aren't you over this grieving yet?"

Again, I found returning to church different each time. Since I was on staff full time at my church, going back after my first husband died seemed easy, even though his funeral had been held there. But as a children's pastor I was in a different section of the church each Sunday and very seldom in the main sanctuary. However, things were different after my second husband died. I was still on staff but as a volunteer. My second husband's funeral had been held at another church, one with a larger sanctuary. I found going to church to be difficult. It took me a good while before I made it to every service. I am very thankful for my pastor and congregation who said to me, "We want you healthy when you come through this, whatever it takes." They never judged me and never scolded me for being absent from services.

How I wish that for all of you. You will know when you feel like returning to church. You may wish to enlist a friend to go along with you so you do not have to enter by yourself. You may even wish for someone to pave the way and field all the questions, as your thoughts are likely to be, *Just let me come in, sit down, and enjoy, and not have to talk!*

Being in God's house is still very important. "I love the house where you live, O Lord, the place where your glory dwells" (Ps. 26:8 NIV). "One thing I ask of the Lord, this is what I seek; that I may dwell in the house of the Lord all the days of my life, to gaze upon the beauty of the Lord and to seek him in his temple" (Ps. 27:4 NIV). But it can be hard for some to go back after the death of a spouse.

* * * * * * * * * * *

Prayer

Father, bless my friends as they enter Your house of worship. May they be greeted with love, warmth, and caring; allowed their own space to worship You, even if through tears; permitted to just sit, or even leave early; and given time to acclimate to life as a single person among the congregation. In Jesus's name, amen.

* * * * * * * * * * *

Changes, Selling the House, Moving

Please, please, take your time in making major changes if at all possible. Sometimes we think, *If I just get away from this home where my spouse and I lived together so long* or *I have got to get out of here and start a new life,* and then we make major moves and changes that turn out in the long run to not be the best for us. We can wake up one day very unhappy, wishing we had never made that move or change!

In those early months, we are not thinking clearly. Our thinking is muddled in grief, which means that making good decisions is almost impossible. It is advised that we not make any major changes in the first year after our loss.

In the hospital before my second husband passed, I told the family I would be moving soon. I was an eight-hour drive away from most of my family. (My son and his family lived four hours away, but everyone else was farther.) I felt like I had no reason to stay where I was, but

I stayed another twenty months. And I am very glad I did. When I did make the move, I knew it was what I needed to do—and I was at peace with the change.

For some, it may be possible to wait, but for others, a change is imminent because of health or other reasons. I pray that God will give you His peace and hope in the midst of your change. I pray that you will have patient family members and friends who will come alongside you and help you make the change. With so much changing so fast, remember that God is faithful and will be with you always. He will never leave you! He will go with you wherever you go!

"The Lord will watch over your life. The Lord will watch over your coming and going both now and forevermore" (Ps. 121:7–8 NIV).

* * * * * * * * * * *

Prayer
Father, bless those who have suffered loss as they make their transition, be it from one house to another, from a house to a care facility, or from city to city. May You fill each grieving spouse with hope for his or her future. In Jesus's name, amen.

● ● ● ● ● ● ● ● ● ● ●

Why Am I Still Here?

I recently listened to a woman whom doctors previously thought would be dead by the time she was sixteen years of age. She is now in her fifties and has been in a wheelchair for many years. Having seen many of her friends pass on, she tearfully asked, "Why am I still here?" Her question continued, "Why do those who are seemingly healthier pass on while I am still here?" The only answer that makes sense to me is, *"God still has a purpose for you!* Your time to pass on has not arrived yet!"

As you think about the passing of your spouse, do you ever wonder why your spouse passed and you are still here? In my case, both of my spouses were younger than I was. Some things just don't make sense. But there is a bigger question: what will you do with the life you have left? You are still here! God has kept you here for a purpose.

It has now been thirty months since my second husband passed. As I mentioned in the previous section, I did not make any major changes (transitions) right away.

In fact, it was twenty months before I made the change. But through my transition, I began to find my purpose. My purpose has become a part of my healing. I have been an ordained minister for several years. In my new community, I have been hired as an associate pastor. I am finding healing as I minister to the hurting people in my new community! Doing for others is one of the best ways to find real healing and purpose! There is a feeling of hope that comes as you do for others. (But may I add that you should give help in moderation. You are still healing yourself!)

• • • • • • • • • • •

Prayer

Father, You have a purpose for each of us. We don't understand why our spouses are gone while we are still here. I ask in the name of Jesus that You will guide each of us to find Your best for our futures—hope! May You open the right doors for us to *find and fulfill* our purposes. No matter our ages, You have something for each of us to do! Amen.

The Presence

As I was teaching my grandchildren a song one Easter evening, I felt a familiar presence enter the room. I could not see the face, but I recognized the body. It was my second husband. If someone would have told me a story like this one before that Easter evening, I would have been very skeptical. I would have said, "That can't happen." But now that I have experienced it, all I can say is that somehow it happens. (My grandchildren did not act as if anything strange had taken place. The visitation was just for me!)

Here is another story. My husband always wore the same cologne. In fact, after he would play with our grandchildren, they always smelled like Grandpa Dave. The youngest was only eighteen months when Grandpa Dave passed away, but at four years old, she still has a connection to him. She will ask to smell the bottle, give a wide grin, and say, "Grandpa Dave."

This scent has become important to all of us. Many times as I walked through a certain place in our home after Dave was gone, I would catch a whiff of that cologne. When I would back up to smell it again, the fragrance would be gone. I would stop and just stand there. I felt close to him. It was not a daily or even weekly occurrence. It would just happen suddenly, and then it was gone.

For you, it may have been a dream that included your spouse. A widow friend said that one night she asked God to send her a hug from her husband. That night she dreamed about her husband, and in the dream he gave her a hug.

Some have said they saw their spouses walking down the street or sensed their spouses' presences close to them.

I cannot explain these events, but I am very thankful that God gives us these glimpses—and no, we are not crazy!

● ● ● ● ● ● ● ● ● ● ●

Prayer

Father, thank You for the ways in which You reach out to comfort us in our grief and loss. Bless my grieving friends with more glimpses of their departed spouses! In Jesus's name, amen.

❂ ❂ ❂ ❂ ❂ ❂ ❂ ❂ ❂ ❂

Cleaning Out the Closet

Cleaning out the closet seems to bring a stronger sense of finality to your loss. Until the time you remove your deceased spouse's clothes from the closet, there seems to be the possibility your spouse will come back home. It is like he or she is just on a trip or spending a few days with the grandchildren. But when the personal items, his or her clothes, are gone, it is more real that he or she is gone!

I decided to clean out the closet because I needed to downsize and be better prepared for the change that would eventually come for me. I thought of it this way: My husband was a giver. He would give you his last dollar if you needed it. When I put his clothes out in the garage sale, I priced them reasonably. I knew he would want them to be used by those who needed them. In fact, one woman looked at his shorts and thought of her husband. "I can't afford to purchase all of these," she said.

I told her, "Take them, and give me what you can!" I

knew I was doing what my spouse would want me to do, and that was comforting to me.

My mother passed away a little over a year ago. As I help my father each week, I see a job that he is not ready to do. Mom had two closets crammed full of clothes. Someday when my father is ready, I will help him sort, sell, and/or give away those clothes. Until then, he keeps the closet doors closed.

Some people, as they are doing this task, choose to be creative in what they do with the clothing. I have seen favorite shirts made into pillows or even quilts. For my stepchildren, I kept clothing that they had purchased for their dad or that had sports logos that were important between them. I gave my stepdaughter her father's DJ tuxedo because the last wedding her father DJ'd was her best friend's.

Cleaning out your spouse's closet is something that eventually will need to be done, but the timing is important. Hopefully, you will be able to do this task in your own time and in your own way, and it will bring comfort and hope to you.

* * * * * * * * * * *

Prayer

Father, as these grieving spouses go through the tasks that are before them, may they find comfort and hope as they share their spouses' personal items with others. In Jesus's name, amen.

* * * * * * * * * *

Who Am I Now?

For a number of years, you and your spouse were a team. Much of who you are now is the result of that special someone whom you lived with and worked alongside. Now it is just you. There is a big part of you that is missing.

Maybe you and your spouse loved dancing, but how do you dance as one? Maybe you enjoyed attending concerts together, but now even thinking of going to a concert leaves you feeling lonely. Or what about those Friday night dinners out together? It is very hard to sit in a restaurant booth across from an empty spot. Going out with another couple used to be a lot of fun, and you really looked forward to those times, but now it is just the three of you. Seeing the other couple together is a reminder of your painful loss.

So who am I now? Well, I am alone. I now have the title "widow" or "widower"—something that is depressing to think about. I love the following passage of God's Word:

Though I walk in the midst of trouble, you preserve my life. You stretch out your hand ... and with your right hand you save me. The Lord will fulfill his purpose for me. ... O Lord, you know me. You know when I sit and when I rise; you perceive my thoughts from afar. You discern my going out and my lying down; you are familiar with all of my ways. ... You hem me in—behind and before; you have laid your hand on me. (Ps. 138:7–8, 139:1–5 NIV)

Who are you? You are known by God completely. He knows where you are and what you are going through. "How precious to me are your thoughts, O God. How vast is the sum of them. Were I to count them, they would outnumber the grains of sand. When I awake, I am still with you" (Ps. 139:17 NIV). What a wonderful, true, and hopeful thought! I wonder how many grains of sand would equal the number of thoughts God has just about you!

* * * * * * * * * * *

Prayer

Father, guide us to see the picture of who we are in You. Bring alongside each of these bereaved spouses people who will let them develop who they are now at their own pace and in their own ways. Never let us lose sight of who we are in You, Lord. In Jesus's name, amen.

Laughing Again

Many times as I have sat down with a family following the loss of a loved one and before preparing the funeral sermon, I have found the family telling me story after story about their loved one. As they share memories that are very precious to them, the laughter begins, mingling with tears. This is a very healthy atmosphere.

But I have also witnessed a remaining spouse who, upon laughing, will say, "Oh, here I am laughing," meaning that the person believes that laughing is a wrong thing for him or her to be doing. I find myself assuring such people that laughing is not wrong. It is, as a matter of fact, really good for them.

In the book of Proverbs, we read these words: "A cheerful heart makes you healthy, but a broken spirit dries you up" (Prov. 17:22 NIRV). Although it is hard for us to be truly happy during our grief, it is good for us to laugh. Laughing relieves stress, improves our moods, and even relieves pain. After a good laugh, we do feel better. Right?

Let your mind remember those memories that bring laughter. Remember something you and your spouse did together that, every time you talk about the experience, brings a hearty belly laugh. This is healthy. Think about the most embarrassing moment you and your spouse ever had and laugh. Again, this is healthy. What about your children and even your grandchildren? I know there are remembrances that will bring smiles and laughter from them.

Laughter is an important part of grieving! The last part of the above-mentioned verse in a different Bible translation reads, "But a broken spirit drains your strength" (Prov. 17:22 NCV). What a comparison! Laughter—a cheerful heart—makes you healthy, compared to not laughing, which results in a broken spirit, which in turn leaves you dried up, weak, and depressed.

It is okay to laugh. Laughter will help you to feel hope!

❂ ❂ ❂ ❂ ❂ ❂ ❂ ❂ ❂ ❂ ❂

Prayer
Father, thank You for the experience of laughter. You gave us the emotion of merriment as a good medicine. May we laugh out loud and not feel guilty. May we again feel and see humor as a part of our lives. In Jesus's name, amen.

"You Are Not Over This Yet?"

* * * * * * * * *

In our society today, I find that people do not understand grief unless they have experienced it firsthand. After your spouse dies, well-meaning people may ask you, "Are you still grieving?", adding, "It's been six months. You should be over this and moving on."

I sent a message today to a mother who lost a young child to cancer several months ago. My message read, "How are you and your family doing? Grief is so hard. You came to my mind today. I want to let you know you are loved and prayed for today!" I had had this mother in my classroom when she was in second grade. Her response to me was, "Thank you so much, Mrs. S. It is really so hard. Your message means a lot!"

One day after I lost my second husband, a friend approached me. I knew she was ready to say, "Suck it up, buttercup!" I actually put my hand in front of her face, saying, "Don't go there!" I knew I was not ready to hear her advice to suck it up and move on. And yes, she is still a very dear friend!

Don't be afraid to stand up for yourself. No one but you knows how you feel. No one but you knows where you are in your grief. No one but you knows what is best for you at this moment.

Be open with your family, friends, and coworkers. They don't mean to hurt you, but many times they are at a loss when it comes to what to say or do. You can help them by giving them ideas of ways they could help you. I have found that people around me really appreciated me sharing things like, "I really cannot go out to dinner with a couple right now," or "Yes, a Starbucks would taste pretty good right now," or "I cannot go there with you because it brings back too many memories." I think you get the idea. Just be kind and honest.

In the Word, we read of a friend: "A friend loves you all the time. A brother [or sister] is born for adversity" (Prov. 17:17 NIV).

* * * * * * * * * *

Prayer
Father, thank You for the many friends that we have and for the way they care for us. Please help us to communicate our needs. May our friends understand when we do not accept an invitation because of our grief. In Jesus's name, amen.

When Will Everything Be Normal Again?

● ● ● ● ● ● ● ● ● ●

Sorry to say, but nothing will return to the old normal. A person is gone from the normal group. What was normal once will never be exactly that way again.

This may sound sad. It is sad. But hopefully, as you work your way through your grief, you will find your new normal. It will be different in some ways. It may entail living in a different house or a different city; remarrying and having a blended family; choosing a different occupation; and maybe even going back to school. Whatever your new normal looks like, embrace it and give it your best.

As I have gone through my life, I have had several new normals. Each time I have found myself calling that period of my life my new chapter. I feel like my life is a book with many, many chapters.

So, my friend, what will your next chapter look like? Will you embrace it and make the best of it?

Scripture

In Jeremiah we read these words:

> "I say this because I know what I am planning for you," says the Lord. "I have good plans for you, not plans to hurt you. I will give you hope and a good future. Then you will call my name. You will come to me and pray to me, and I will listen to you. You will search for me. And when you search for me with all your heart, you will find me." (Jer. 29:11–13 NCV)

Prayer

Father, may You, the God of all comfort, give these spouses true comfort and peace in their journeys. May they be surrounded with amazing people who will be to them *exactly* what they need. May they find their hope, peace, and futures wrapped up in You! In Jesus's name, amen.

Special Remembrance Days

• • • • • • • • •

As you go through your grief journey, you will encounter special remembrance days, such as the anniversary of your spouse's passing, his or her birthday, your anniversary, and other days that were special just to you and your spouse. When these days arrive in the years to come, how will you react to them? Will they be routine like any other day, or will you find a way to celebrate them and make them special?

In the past week, I encountered one of those days—the three-year anniversary of Dave's passing. I had planned to engage in ministry, but when that day arrived, I changed my plans. I canceled my ministry, rescheduling it for another day. (I am very thankful to belong to a church filled with people who love me, allow me to grieve, and desire healing for me.) I had a home day. I celebrated that day by reading a book about the Biltmore Estate in Asheville, North Carolina. Dave and I had spent time visiting there. He had even done work on the historic building's roof. As I read, I could picture the many rooms.

I saw Dave and myself touring that huge house. Reading and remembering brought healing to me. When I awoke the next morning, I was ready to continue the work of ministry. What helped me? *I took time to grieve!*

On other special remembrance days, I have gone to a particular restaurant that we frequented, and ordered what we would have ordered had he been there. (Many times we shared an entrée instead of buying two separate ones, so I did not end up with too much food.) Each time, even though I have been alone, I have felt healing happening.

You may not wish to spend these special remembrance days alone. For you, it may be best to have a celebration with family and/or friends. Remember, the goal is to find healing, so whatever is best for you will be the right thing.

Prayer

Father, I pray that You will bring ideas to the minds of these, my friends, so that these special remembrance days will bring healing to their hearts. May those around them give them permission to grieve, and may they continue to heal in the years to come. In Jesus's name, amen.

● ● ● ● ● ● ● ● ● ● ●

Conclusion

We have come to the conclusion of our journey together, but it is not the conclusion of our grief journeys. We will continue to miss that special someone for many days and even years. We will find ourselves returning to our safe spots where we feel close to our departed spouses.

At the beginning of this journey, I asked you to make one important decision: *to allow yourself to grieve.* Have you begun? Do you *desire to be healthy* as you go through the grieving process? What has seemed very hard for you? What has seemed easier?

A word that has become a part of my thoughts is *perseverance.* When I first thought of this word as it related to my life, I thought of my perseverance in my past. Lately, though, I have begun to think of the word in another way. Instead of *perseverance* referring to my past, it has become a word that will lead me to my future. I will persevere to find hope in my future! A scripture that comes to my mind is, "Being confident of this, that he who began a good work in you will carry it on to completion until the day of Christ Jesus" (Phil. 1:6 NIV). God is not finished with me yet! He has a plan for my future!

God is not finished with you either. He has a plan for your future. When the right time arrives, *will you persevere and seek hope for your future?*

In our journeys, if we permit him to, God will redeem our hurt, struggles, and losses, turning them into something good. When we look at Joseph from the book of Genesis, we find him being sold into slavery, bought as a slave, accused falsely, imprisoned, and forgotten about. But God redeemed those struggles so that Joseph was able to save his people from starvation caused by a famine. Joseph persevered and moved toward the future.

You may be screaming, "No way! Good could never come from my loss! It is too great! It hurts too much!" Well, I don't understand it all, but I do know that *God makes a way!* In fact, *Hope for the Grieving Spouse* is a prime example of good coming from my losses. I pray it is a help to you. When you can, look for ways to help others—let good come from bad!

* * * * * * * * * *

Scripture

"I am still confident of this: I will see the goodness of the Lord in the land of the living. Wait for the Lord" (Ps. 27:13–14a NIV).

Prayer

Father God, may You give every grieving spouse the perseverance he or she needs to find hope for his or her future. May they find hope as you redeem their hurt, their pain, and their struggles! May this be done in memory of their departed spouses and to bring honor, glory, and praise to Jesus! Bless each one. I pray this in the name of Jesus. Amen.

Appendix

Tom and Linda Swinderman soon after they were married.

Dave and Linda Cronebaugh on their wedding day.

While writing *Hope for the Grieving Spouse*, I have been praying for each of you. I know from experience how hard this time of your life is. I pray that God will continue to be your source of strength and encouragement as you persevere, moving into the future.

If there is any way I can be an encouragement to you, please feel free to contact me at hopeiscoming2u@outlook.com.

God bless you!

• • • • • • • • • •

Memories

Memories

Memories

Memories

Memories

CPSIA information can be obtained
at www.ICGtesting.com
Printed in the USA
LVHW050451230520
656341LV00003B/447